Ideas Box!

Chocolate

Jillian Powell

Yummy! That's a big slice!

FRANKLIN WATTS
LONDON • SYDNEY

espresso
education

This edition 2013

Franklin Watts
338 Euston Road
London NW1 3BH

Franklin Watts Australia
Level 17/207 Kent Street
Sydney NSW 2000

Text and illustration © Franklin Watts 2011

The Espresso characters are originated
and designed by Claire Underwood and
Pesky Ltd.

The Espresso characters are the property of
Espresso Education Ltd.

A CIP catalogue record for this book is
available from the British Library.

ISBN: 978 1 4451 0398 3
Dewey: 641.3'374

Series Editor: Sarah Peutrill
Art Director: Jonathan Hair
Series Designer: Matthew Lilly
Picture Researcher: Diana Morris
Illustrations by Artful Doodlers Ltd.

Printed in China

PIcture credits:
3445128471/Shutterstock: front cover b.
Aroas/Shutterstock: 16bl. Bloody/
Shutterstock: 1, 27tl. Peter Bowater/
Alamy: 9tr. BrazilPhotos/Alamy: 5t.
ChaosMaker/Shutterstock: 16bc. Martin
Darley/Shutterstock: 27tc. Danita
Delimont/Alamy: 4cr. Digital Genetics/
Shutterstock: 7t. Kentoh/Shutterstock: 18.
Ilkka Kukko/Shutterstock: 23t. Edward H
Menin Gallery, NY/Werner Forman
Archive: 10. Elena Moiseeva/Shutterstock:
27tr. Thomas Mueller/PD: 9tl. Museum of
London/HIP/Topfoto: 14br. Alfredo dagli
Orti/The Art Archive/Alamy: 11t. PHB.cz
(Richard Semik)/Shutterstock: 20b. Ann
Ronan PL/HIP/Topfoto: 15cr. Alex
Staroseltsev/Shutterstock: 19t. Startraks
Photo/Rex Features: 29. Tobik/
Shutterstock: front cover t. Julie
Woodhouse/Alamy: 23b. XuRa/
Shutterstock: 6t.

Every attempt has been made to clear
copyright. Should there be any
inadvertent omission please apply to the
publisher for rectification.

Contents

Where does chocolate come from? 4

How do cacao trees grow? 6

Cacao farming 8

The history of chocolate 10

⬇ Make a collage of the Aztec chocolate god 12

The chocolate trade 14

Make a chocolate piñata 16

⬇ Manufacturing chocolate 18

Is chocolate good for me? 20

Melting chocolate 22

Make chocolate leaves 24

Chocolate recipes 26

⬇ Chocolate heaven 28

Glossary and Activity sheets 30

Espresso connections 31

Index and quiz answers 32

⬇ Pages with this symbol have a downloadable photocopiable sheet (see page 30).

Where does chocolate come from?

Kim has just baked a chocolate cake. Mmm, everyone likes chocolate. Polly likes chocolate ice cream. Eddy likes chocolate biscuits. Ash's favourite book is *Charlie and the Chocolate Factory*. "If only chocolate grew on trees!" he says. "But it does!" Sal tells him.

Karina goes to school in Peru.

Sal's class has been writing letters to pupils at a school in Peru. In Peru they grow cacao beans, from which chocolate is made. Her pen pal, Karina, has told her how farmers grow cacao trees and harvest the beans. The cacao trees sound amazing. They grow up to 18 metres tall and can go on producing beans for over 100 years.

These men are harvesting cacao seed pods.

Kim wants to know what everyone's favourite kind of chocolate is, so he has organised a chocolate tasting. Everyone has to put on a blindfold, taste little pieces of different kinds of chocolate then say which they like best. The bar chart shows which was most popular.

Quiz:
What does the Aztec word chocolate mean?

A) Sweet water

B) Bitter water

C) Sugar water

Quiz answers are on page 32.

5

How do cacao trees grow?

Cacao trees grow in tropical parts of the world in Africa and Asia, and in South and Central America. Sal has written down some interesting facts she has learned about cacao trees!

Harvested cacao pod

What else is interesting?

Interesting Facts

• Cacao trees produce flowers all year round.

• They flower and produce seed pods at the same time. This is very unusual!

• The flowers are so small that only tiny midges can get inside to pollinate them. Once they are pollinated, seeds form in the seed pods.

• The pods grow straight off the trunk and branches. They are about as big as a pineapple and take about six months to grow to that size.

• The pods have a thick shell and cannot open on their own. They need birds, monkeys or 'breakers' working on farms to break into them!

This cacao pod is broken and shows the seeds or beans inside.

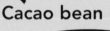

Cacao bean

Science spot: pollination

Pollination is the movement of pollen (a fine powder made by flowers) from one part of a flower to another. Flowers need to be pollinated to form their fruits and seeds. Pollen is moved either by the wind or by insects and other animals. Find out why the small, waxy flowers of cacao trees can only be pollinated by one type of midge.

Quiz:
How many seeds does a cacao pod contain?

A) Up to 50

B) Up to 100

C) Up to 1,000

Cacao farming

Sal has received a letter from her pen pal Karina. Her uncle is a cacao farmer. She describes his farm in her letter.

Dear Sal,

My uncle grows cacao trees on his farm. He also grows rubber, Brazil nuts, limes and chilli peppers. Nearby my uncle's farm there are big plantations where they only grow cacao.

The cacao seedlings are grown in fibre baskets for planting out. It takes the trees about five years before they start to produce pods that contain the beans. When the cacao pods are ripe, they turn red, orange or yellow. The pods are harvested and cut open by hand. The beans are wrapped in banana leaves and they are left to ferment for a few days, which turns them brown and less bitter. Finally they are dried in the Sun and then cleaned before they are bagged up ready for shipping.

Tell me about the area you live in. What foods do the local farms grow?

Love, Karina

Small mixed farms

- Cacao is grown with other crops.
- Farms border the rainforest.
- Trees benefit from natural pesticides and fertilisers.
- Trees remain productive for many years.

A worker checks cacao plants on a large plantation.

This worker is drying cacao beans on a traditional plantation.

Single crop plantations

- Cacao is grown as a single crop.
- The rainforest is cleared for farming.
- Trees require more fertilisers and pesticides.
- Trees remain productive for about ten years.

Kim bought a bar of Fairtrade chocolate. He researched what 'fair trade' means on a website and found that it means the cacao beans have been bought at a fair price from the farmers, and that their farms have good working conditions. The farmers also receive extra money for their communities, for example to build schools and provide fresh water.

Feedback...

What could you do to support fair trade?

The history of chocolate

Sal has prepared a presentation on the history of chocolate for her class. She starts by telling them that people have been eating chocolate for about 150 years, but they have been drinking it for over 1,000 years!

This pot was made by the Mayans. They lived in Central America over 1,000 years ago. The decoration shows people harvesting cacao pods. The Mayans crushed the cacao beans and mixed them with chilli peppers, cornmeal and spices to make a frothy drink.

The Mayans even used cacao beans like money to buy cooking pots, food and clothes. Four beans could buy a pumpkin and ten beans could buy a rabbit!

The Aztecs lived in Mexico 500 years ago. It was too dry to grow cacao trees on the dry highlands there so the beans to make their spicy chocolate drink came from the lowlands. Chocolate was important in Aztec religious ceremonies and they made offerings of the beans to their gods.

The Aztecs thought that drinking chocolate gave you wisdom and power. Only Aztec nobles, priests and rich merchants could afford to drink it. This is the Aztec Emperor Montezuma. He drank about 50 goblets of chocolate every day!

On the map, Ash shows Polly where the Mayans and Aztecs lived in Mexico and Central America. He explains that the Mayan people lived there from about 250 to 900 AD and the Aztecs from the 1100s to the 1500s.

Wow!

USA

MEXICO

Mayans

Aztecs

Make a collage of the Aztec chocolate god

Kim and Ash have learned that the Aztecs believed that the god Quetzalcoatl brought cacao trees from Paradise and taught the Aztecs how to make chocolate. They have made a collage of the Aztec chocolate god using chocolate and sweet wrappers.

Quetzalcoatl

1 Decide how big your collage is going to be. Print off a picture of the Aztec chocolate god to the size you want.

You will need:

- Picture of Quetzalcoatl
- Large sheet of card
- Tracing paper and pencil
- Scissors and glue
- Assorted chocolate and sweet wrappers

2 Trace the outline onto the sheet of card using the tracing paper.

3 Roughly decide how you are going to arrange the wrappers to cover the shape of the god. Try to get a nice mix of colours.

4 Begin cutting wrappers to stick onto the outline. Work around the edges first to get the shape of the god.

5 Cut and stick more wrappers until you have filled in the middle part.

Be crafty

You can use any part of the wrappers including the words as well as the colours and pictures. You could also try making a collage of another Aztec god, like the god of farming, using pictures of crops the Aztecs grew such as corn, tomatoes and peppers.

The chocolate trade

Ash has researched and made a timeline to show how chocolate came to Europe after the Spanish conquered Mexico in the 1500s and began to ship back goods, including cacao beans.

1521 Hernán Cortés conquers Mexico and brings cacao beans back to Spain.

1600s-1800s European countries establish plantations to grow cacao, using slave labour from Africa.

1657 The first chocolate house opens in London.

1700s Steam-powered machines used to grind cacao beans.

1765 First chocolate factory in the USA.

A timeline is a list of related events arranged in order by the date on which they happened.

Chocolate houses were places to meet and gossip over a hot chocolate.

1828 Invention of the cocoa press.

1847 First chocolate bar made by Fry & Sons, Bristol, England.

1875 Swiss introduce milk chocolate.

1879 George Cadbury builds Bournville village for his workers.

2006 Chocolate is a £48 billion industry worldwide.

History spot: Bournville

In 1879 George Cadbury of the Cadbury chocolate company built a new factory, called Bournville, near Birmingham in the UK. He then built a village for his workers, including houses (right), shops and schools. Find out more about the Bournville village and how the Cadbury family looked after their employees, or find out about the companies Rowntree, Terry's of York or Hershey in the USA.

This is my favourite chocolate!

Feedback...

How many chocolate brands can you name and which is your favourite? Think about the way it is packaged and advertised. Does that encourage you to buy it or is it just the taste?

Make a chocolate piñata

Sal and Ash have made a Mexican piñata for chocolate treats. They read that the Mayans and Aztecs made piñatas from clay pots for games and religious ceremonies. Polly and Eddy want to be first to have a go at breaking the piñata!

You will need:

- A large balloon
- Newspaper
- Flour and water paste (1:2 parts flour/water)
- Crepe paper
- Glue
- String
- Chocolate sweets

1 Blow up the balloon. Dip strips of newspaper into the paste and stick them onto the balloon vertically, leaving a hole around the top. Allow them to dry and then repeat with horizontal strips.

2 Pop the balloon and pull it out through the hole. Cut the crepe paper into zigzags, semi circles and other Aztec designs.

3 Glue on the crepe paper to decorate the piñata. If you prefer you can make it into a bird or animal design, and add streamers to represent fur or feathers.

4 Make four small holes around the top and thread through a piece of string. Tie a longer piece of string to the first piece to hang it up.

5 Fill the piñata with some chocolate treats and then hang it up over a tablecloth or sheet to play the piñata game.

Play the game!

Each player takes turns to try to break the piñata. Blindfold the first player and give them a bat or stick. Spin them round three times to leave them facing the piñata. Players continue taking turns until the piñata breaks, then the winner shares out the treats.

Manufacturing chocolate

Sal's class has been on a visit to a chocolate factory to see how chocolate is made today. She has filled in a worksheet recording what they learned.

How long does it take to make a chocolate bar?

Between two and four days

How many types of cacao bean are used in one bar of chocolate?

Up to 12 types

What ingredients did you see being used today?

Cacao beans   sugar   milk   caramel   nuts

Describe the main stages in chocolate-making that you saw:

1. Giant ovens roast the cacao beans.
2. The beans are cracked and the 'nibs' inside them are ground into chocolate liquor.
3. Giant presses squeeze the cocoa butter out of the liquor.
4. Steel rollers blend cocoa butter and liquor with milk and sugar to make chocolate.
5. The chocolate is heated and cooled in conching and tempering machines.
6. Machines pour the chocolate into moulds or use it to coat caramel or nuts.
7. Machines wrap the chocolate.

This machine is mixing the chocolate.

Sal asked a worker this question:

Why do you heat and cool the chocolate so many times?

Conching and tempering makes the chocolate silky and 'fondant' which means it stays solid at room temperature, but melts in the warmth of your mouth. Some chocolate is conched for up to six days!

Quiz:
How many cacao beans do you need to make a 450g bar of chocolate?

A) 400

B) 1,000

C) A million

Science spot: cosmetics

Chocolate is used as an ingredient in cosmetics and medicines. Find out how it is used.

Is chocolate good for me?

At the factory, Sal has learned some interesting facts about chocolate as food. She has written a report about it for her school newspaper.

Chocolate report

Espresso Extra

Chocolate: a feel good food!

Did you know that chocolate contains over 300 chemicals and some may make you feel more alert or cheer you up? Chemicals like theobromine can increase the activity of your brain cells.

Is chocolate healthy?

Chocolate also contains flavenoids and antioxidants which may protect the body against damage and ageing. Dark chocolate contains over twice as many antioxidants as milk chocolate – and fewer calories!

Chocolate also contains sugar, a kind of carbohydrate that is high in calories. It gives you energy but can also make you put on weight. Sugar also attacks the enamel on your teeth if you don't brush them regularly. Finally, the cocoa butter in chocolate contains saturated fats, and you should only eat these in small amounts. However, it also contains healthy fats like oleic acid. So, as long as you don't eat too much of it, chocolate really can be good for you!

Theobromine is poisonous to dogs and cats so eating chocolate can harm and even kill them. Never give your pet chocolate, except for the special pet brands.

Kim has made a bar chart showing how long it takes to burn off the calories in a small chocolate bar.

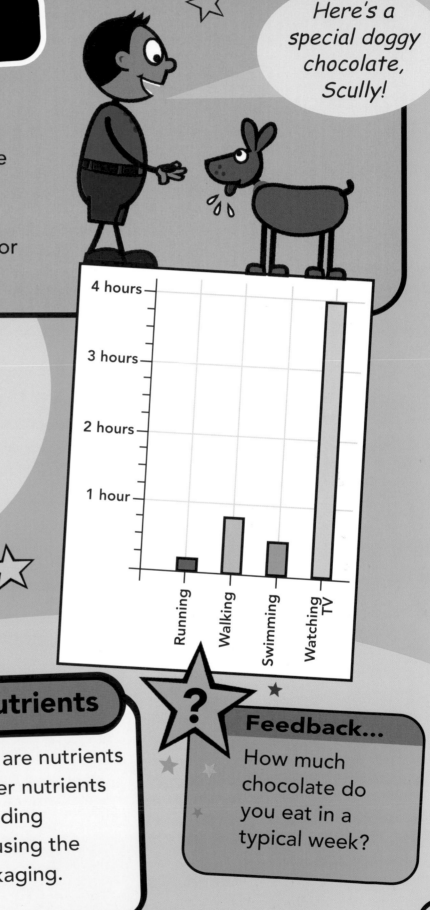

Here's a special doggy chocolate, Scully!

4 hours
3 hours
2 hours
1 hour

Running
Walking
Swimming
Watching TV

Science spot: nutrients

Carbohydrates and fats are nutrients in food. Investigate other nutrients found in chocolate including vitamins and minerals, using the information on the packaging.

?

Feedback...

How much chocolate do you eat in a typical week?

Melting chocolate

Kim has been doing an experiment to find out what happens when you heat chocolate. Polly is helping him to clean up! This is Kim's record of what happened.

What we used:
- A bar of chocolate
- A foil tray
- A star mould
- A candle
- Tongs

What we did
We broke the chocolate into small pieces and put it into one of the foil trays. We lit the candle and, using some tongs, carefully held the tray over it.

Our results
As the flame began to warm the tray, the chocolate began to bubble and soften. It became runny and turned from solid to liquid. When it had all melted, we poured the runny chocolate into the star mould. We left it to cool, and after a while it had become solid again. We had made a chocolate star.

What we learned

Chocolate melts and becomes runny or liquid when it is heated, and turns solid again when it is cooled. This is because the crystals in the cocoa butter loosen when they are heated, and join together when they are cooled. This is important in manufacturing because heating and cooling chocolate improves the texture and make it silky and glossy. It also means that the melted chocolate can be made into lots of different shapes.

This chocolate has been moulded into an Easter bunny.

If you try Kim's experiment, ask an adult to help you heat the chocolate.

Science and Maths spot: melting

Chocolate must be gently heated or it can burn or go lumpy. Heating it in a bowl over hot water works well.

Different types of chocolate have different melting points. Investigate which chocolate (milk, dark or white) melts fastest and organise your data into a graph. You can try timed tests using different melting methods, such as in a bowl over hot water, in your school bag or in the sunshine, or even in your mouth!

Make chocolate leaves

Kim and Polly have been making chocolate leaves using melted chocolate. Eddy wants to try one.

You will need:

- Some leaves
- Kitchen paper
- Saucepan, spoon and bowl
- Baking paper
- Baking tray
- A paintbrush
- White, milk or dark moulding chocolate
- An adult to help you with the cooking

1 Carefully wash and dry the leaves on kitchen paper. Only use non-poisonous plants like rose and camellia to make chocolate leaves. Always check with an adult first!

2 Break the chocolate into small pieces and place in a bowl over a pan of hot water. Stir until the chocolate is melted.

3 Use the paintbrush to brush a thick coat of chocolate (up to about 3 mm) onto the back of each leaf. Be careful not to go over the edges and if you do, tidy them up.

4 Place the leaves on a baking tray or dish lined with baking paper. Put it in the fridge and leave to set.

5 When the chocolate has set, carefully peel each leaf away, starting at the stem end. Make sure you don't eat the leaf!

Crafty cooks

You can make coloured leaves by adding a few drops of food colouring to white chocolate. You could also try adding flavourings such as peppermint or lemon. Use your leaves to decorate cakes or design and make packaging for them as chocolate treats. You can also use melted moulding chocolate for other treats like chocolate-dipped strawberries or cherries.

Chocolate recipes

Kim has baked some chocolate flapjacks. He has written the recipe down in his recipe book with some ideas of his own for next time.

I could use dried apricots next time.

Recipe name: Chocolate cherry flapjacks

Preparation time: 10 minutes

Cooking time: 20–25 minutes

If you try Kim's recipe, ask an adult to help you with the cooking parts.

What you need:

75 g butter

50 g light soft brown sugar

20 g dark or white chocolate chips

30 ml golden syrup

2 tablespoons cocoa powder

175 g porridge oats

20 g dried cherries

SYR

Step-by-step method:

- Pre-heat the oven to 180°C, 350°F, gas mark 4.
- Grease a 20 cm square baking tin and line with greaseproof paper.
- Melt the butter over a low heat, then stir in the golden syrup and sugar until they are dissolved.

Yummy flapjacks Kim!

- Mix in the rest of the ingredients and stir well.
- Pour the mix into the baking tin and pat down with the back of a spoon.
- Bake for 20–25 minutes and then turn out of the tin and allow to cool. Cut into squares (makes about 8–10 flapjacks).

Famous chocolate dishes from around the world

Sachertorte
Viennese chocolate cake with apricot jam and chocolate icing

Black forest gâteau
German chocolate cake with cherries and whipped cream

Chocolate brownies
Chocolate cake squares invented in the USA

Quiz:
Which nation eats the most chocolate every year?

?

Feedback...
What is your favourite chocolate dish or recipe?

A) The United States

B) The United Kingdom

C) Switzerland

Chocolate heaven

Ash has been on a visit to the Roald Dahl Museum as *Charlie and the Chocolate Factory* is his favourite book. He has written about his visit in his diary.

Tuesday 5th

I went to the Roald Dahl Museum today. It was brilliant. I learned all about how Dahl got his idea for *Charlie and the Chocolate Factory* when he was at school and factories used to send out chocolate bars for pupils to test. I wish they did that now! We toured a replica of his writing hut. On the desk there is a silver ball as big as a cannon ball that is made out of chocolate wrappers. I got to dress up as Willy Wonka and then we watched a video.

I learned that Dahl loved chocolates and sweets all his life and kept a big jar by his bedside. Before we left, we went to Café Twit and I bought a chocolate bar!

Here is a scrapbook of ideas for some more places to go and things to see if you love chocolate.

Visit the Chocolate Festival in Turin, Italy. The chocolate-loving Swiss also hold a festival at Versoix every year.

Visit a chocolate factory like Cadbury World, at Bournville, Birmingham.

Take a tour of the Museum of Chocolate in Barcelona, Spain.

Try 12 kinds of hot chocolate at Café Cocoa, Walkers Chocolate Emporium, Ilfracombe, Devon.

food network

Find out about the world's most amazing chocolate sculptures such as this model of a famous New York skyscraper made from over 1,000 kilograms of chocolate and standing 6.6 metres tall!

Wow!

A chef created this chocolate sculpture in 2006. It was the tallest in the world at the time.

Glossary

antioxidants Substances found in dark chocolate and some fruit and vegetables that are believed to protect the body's cells against damage and ageing.

calories Units of energy value in food. A food that is high in calories gives us lots of energy but it may make us put on weight.

cocoa press A machine for extracting cocoa butter from chocolate liquor.

conching Refining chocolate by heating and rolling.

cosmetics Beauty products.

enamel Hard glossy covering on teeth.

ferment To undergo changes as sugars break down.

fertilisers Natural or chemical agents to boost plant growth.

fibre Plant material that can be woven.

flavenoids Chemicals found in foods including dark chocolate and blueberries which may help to protect against heart disease.

humidity Moisture in the air.

midges Small winged insects.

pesticides Natural or chemical agents to control pests.

piñata A hanging pot or mould filled with sweets.

plantation Farm or estate in tropical or semi-tropical countries.

pollinate To carry pollen from the male to the female part of a flower and fertilise it.

pulp Soft, fleshy plant material.

rainforest A tropical forest of mainly evergreen trees.

saturated fats Fats found in foods, including meat and dairy produce, that can make the blood sticky.

seed pod Part of a plant that holds and protects its seeds.

tempering The process of heating and cooling chocolate to make it silky.

theobromine A chemical found in cacao, named from the Greek word for the cacao tree which means 'food of the gods'.

Activity sheets

Go to www.franklinwatts.co.uk/downloads for free activity sheets.

Page 12: A template for Quetzalcoatl.

Page 18: Questions for your own chocolate factory visit.

Page 28: A template for writing your own diary.

Espresso connections

Here are a few ideas for ways you can explore the contents of this book further using Espresso. There are many more resources on chocolate and sweets, including videos in the news archive and news bites.

Where does chocolate come from? (pages 4–7)

Learn where foods, including chocolate, come from in the *Activity arcade* in the *Harvest and food resource box > Farming and growing* in *Science 2*.

Cacao farming (pages 8–9)

Find out more about fair trade with a video on the boom in sale of Fairtrade products and a news report about Fairtrade chocolate being used to make Kit Kats in the *News archive* in *PSHE and Citizenship 2 > World citizenship*.

The history of chocolate (pages 10–11)

Check out a video about Tudor explorers bringing back new foodstuffs to Europe including cacao beans in *History 2 > Tudors > Events*.

Manufacturing chocolate (pages 18–19)

Check out how chocolate packaging now offers nutritional information and advice in the *News archive > Labelling* in *Science 2*.

Is chocolate good for me? (pages 20–21)

Investigate a report in the news archive on how chocolate might help cure coughs in the *News archive > Food and Nutrition* in *Science 2*.

Melting chocolate (pages 22–23)

Watch an experiment about heating and cooling chocolate in *Science 2 > Investigating change > Experiments in the classroom*.

Chocolate recipes (pages 26–27)

Cook with chocolate to celebrate Easter! Make chocolate crispy nests in *D&T 2 > News archive > Making*. Watch a video showing how to make a giant chocolate Easter bunny using a mould in the *News archive > Science 1 > Food*.

Chocolate heaven (pages 28–29)

Watch video clips about Roald Dahl and his love of chocolate in *English 2 > Roald Dahl*. Then invent a new chocolate treat for Willy Wonka and design a poster to market it in *Things to do* in *Roald Dahl*.

Index

antioxidants 20
Aztecs 5, 11, 12, 13, 16

Bournville 15, 29

cacao beans 4, 7, 8, 9, 10, 11, 14, 15, 18, 19
cacao farmers 4, 8–9
cacao (seed) pods 5, 6, 7, 8, 10
cacao trees 4, 6–7, 8, 11, 12
Cadbury 15, 29
calories 20, 21
Central America 6, 10, 11
Charlie and the Chocolate Factory 4, 28
chocolate drinks 10, 11, 14
chocolate houses 14
chocolate liquor 18
chocolate sculptures 29
chocolate tasting 5

chocolate trade 14–15
cocoa butter 18, 20, 23
cocoa press 14, 18
conching 18, 19
Cortés, Hernán 14

Emperor Montezuma 11

factories 14, 15, 18, 20, 28
fairtrade 9
fertilisers 9
flavenoids 20
Fry and Sons 15

gods 11, 12, 13

health facts 20–21
Hershey 15
history of chocolate 10–11

make chocolate leaves 24–25
make a collage 12–13
make a piñata 16–17
making chocolate 18–19, 23
manufacturers 15, 18

Mayans 10, 11, 16
melting chocolate 22–25
Mexico 11, 14, 16

nutrients 21

packaging 15, 21, 25
Peru 4, 8
pesticides 9
places to visit 29
plantations 8, 9, 14
pollination 6, 7

Quetzalcoatl 12

recipes 26–27
religious ceremonies 11, 16
Roald Dahl Museum 28
Rowntree 15

slaves 14
Spain 14, 29

tempering 18, 19
Terry's of York 15
theobromine 20, 21
timeline 14–15

Quiz answers

Page 5: B) The raw cacao beans have a bitter taste
Page 7: A) Between 30 - 50
Page 19: A) 400
Page 27: C) Switzerland